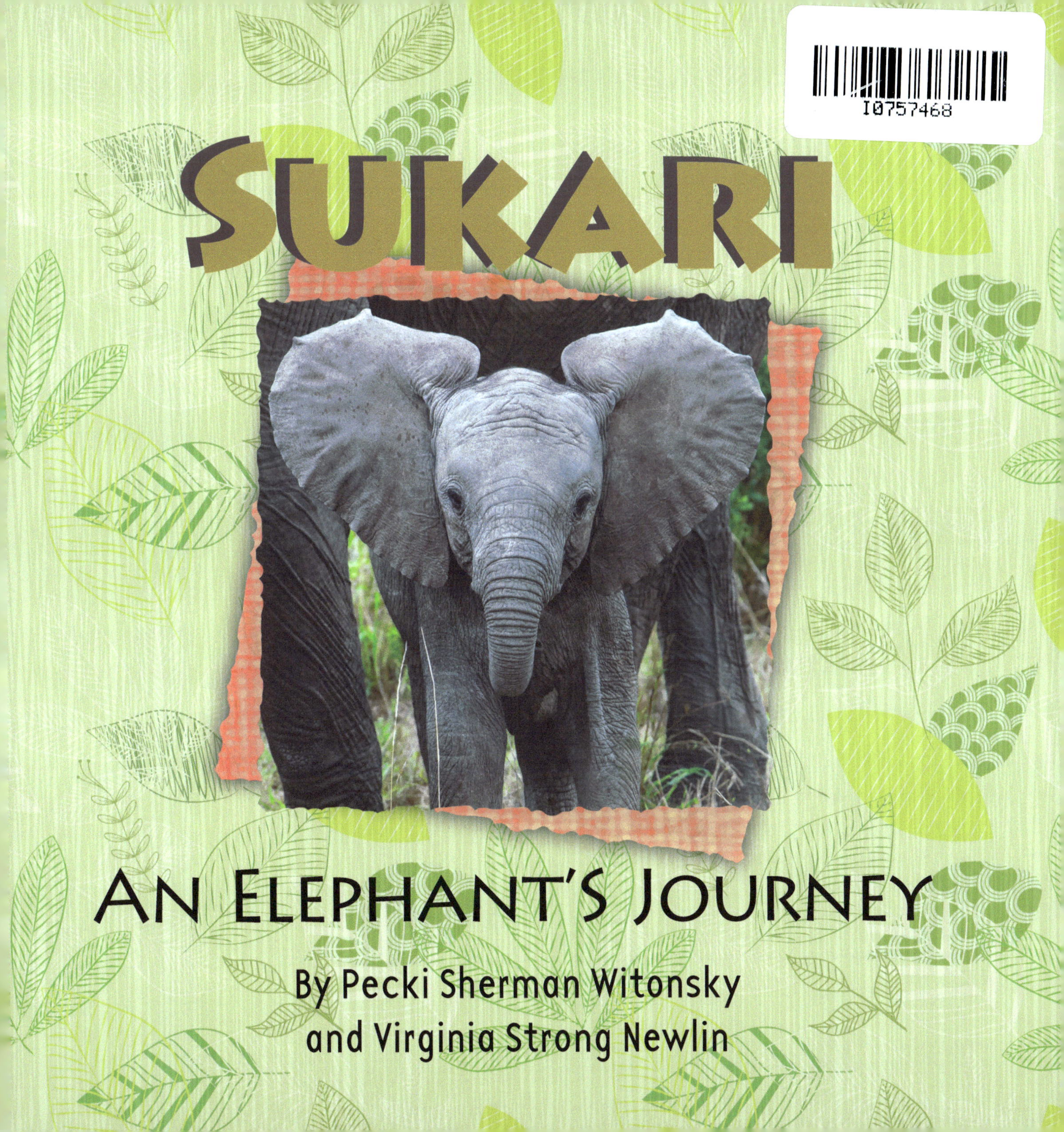

SUKARI
AN ELEPHANT'S JOURNEY
By Pecki Sherman Witonsky
and Virginia Strong Newlin

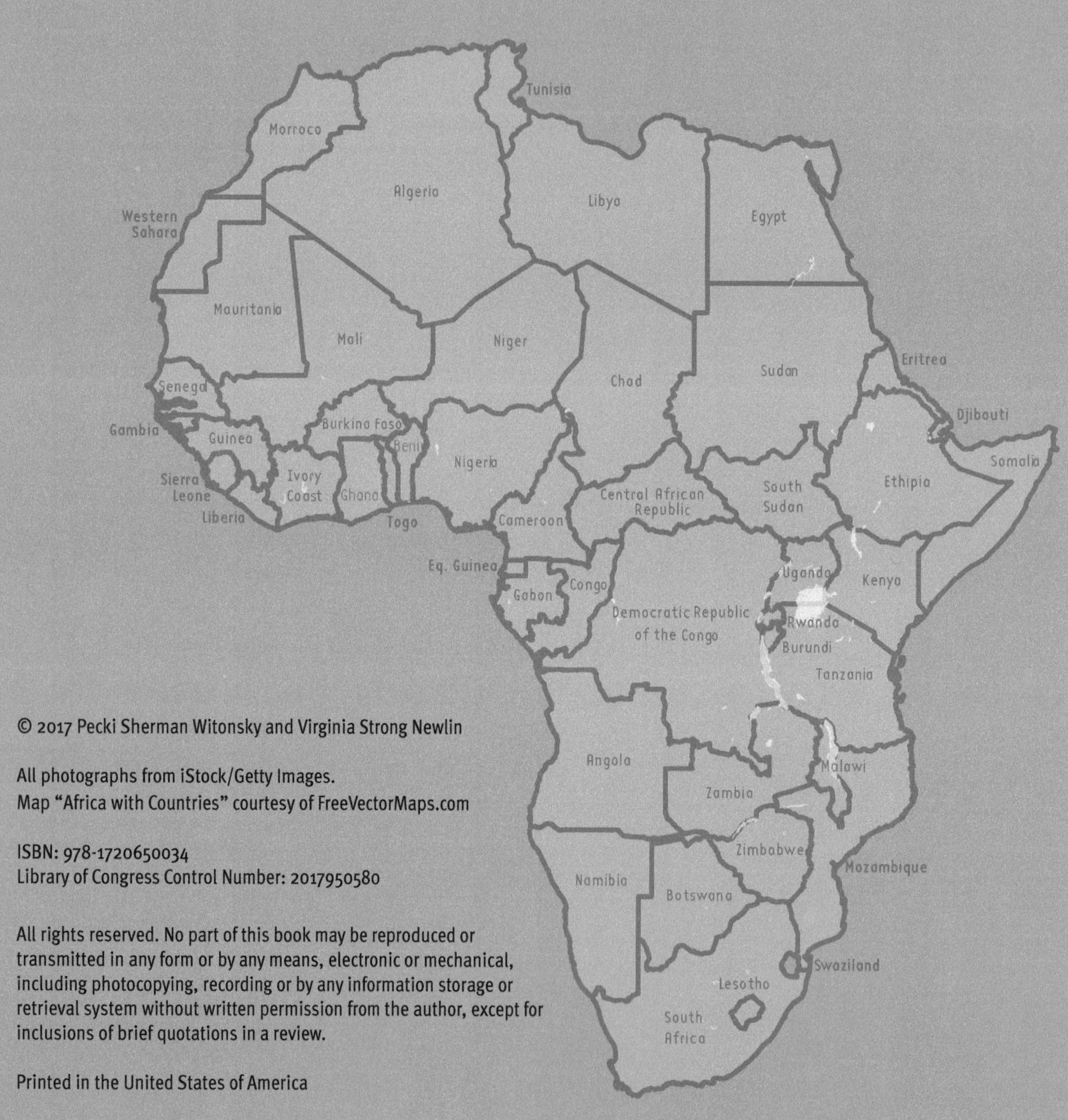

All photographs from iStock/Getty Images.
Map "Africa with Countries" courtesy of FreeVectorMaps.com

ISBN: 978-1720650034
Library of Congress Control Number: 2017950580

Printed in the United States of America

FOREWORD

One January evening in 2015, while watching Bill Maher, I was stunned as he interviewed Kathryn Bigelow who talked about her video, LAST DAYS. She spoke about the mass slaughter of elephants and how the illegal sale of elephant ivory funds terrorist organizations in Africa and around the world.

Seeing this interview reminded me of a safari trip to Kenya with my young son thirty plus years ago. While there we fell in love with the elephants. These magnificent beings seemed to speak to each other as they moved from water hole to water hole. We did learn about poachers, as horrible as it was, but then it was a few bad guys with guns. Today the poachers are soldiers in murderous armies that illegally hunt elephants, kill them, and sell their ivory on the black market.

Some time later, after the safari trip, Virginia Newlin and I wrote a children's story about a girl elephant – Sukari. Life got in the way and Sukari ended up in a drawer. It is time to take her out of the drawer.

Now Sukari can tell her story of elephant love and family devotion.

Now she will bring additional awareness to the plight of the African elephant.

IN EAST AFRICA during the dry season food is scarce.
Elephant families graze apart so there will be food for all.

Now that the rains have come they could feed together.

Sukari, which means sugar in Swahili, followed Zuri her beautiful mother and her grandmother Bibi to the good grass place. Bibi was the matriarch of the herd. She knew the way.

It was a long walk. They would not get there until dark. In the morning there would be fresh grasses and water, a mud wallow, and new friends to play with.

Sukari felt a thump on her
back. It was Moja. He was
her cousin and thirteen
years old— almost grown up
enough to go and live with
the bulls.

"I know where there's lots
of good food." said Moja.

Because Sukari was
still hungry, she asked,
"Where?"

"Over there by the people's camp."

Sukari liked Moja but sometimes he got her into trouble.

"We shouldn't go. Bibi says they will try to hurt us.
Besides Asha, your mother, will see us."

"My mother is talking to grandmother Bibi.
Now's our chance. We'll catch up before she misses us."
Moja nudged Sukari toward the bushes.

"Oh, all right," Sukari said.

They trotted quickly toward the people's camp. Moja looked around but didn't see anyone. He found the place where they threw away spoiled food. In the middle of the heap was an open plastic bag and over-ripe bananas. He gobbled one quickly, then turned and gave one to Sukari.

It tasted good, but she was frightened. "We have to go," said Sukari.

Moja stuffed the rest of the bananas, bag and all, into his mouth and reluctantly followed her back to the herd.

After a while, Sukari saw that Moja was walking very slowly. Asha, Moja's mother, noticed, too. She trumpeted for him to move faster, but he couldn't. Sukari and Asha dropped back to see what was wrong.

"My stomach hurts and there's something in my throat," gasped Moja.

"What have you been
eating?" asked Asha.

"Nothing." Moja coughed.

"He ate a whole bunch of
bananas and a shiny bag,"
Sukari said.

"Tattle-trunk!"

Moja glared at Sukari and
moaned. Then his legs
folded and he collapsed.

"Get up Moja," said Asha.
But he only flopped one ear and groaned.

Asha trumpeted to the herd to stop. Bibi and Zuri,
Sukari's mother, hurried back to them. Asha told them
about the bananas and the shiny bag.

Zuri and Bibi wedged
their ivory tusks and
powerful trunks under
Moja and lifted him.

Then Bibi gave Moja a
wallop on the ribs.

He coughed up the plastic bag,
stood on his tottering legs,
and finally breathed deeply.

"There are bitter grasses in the good grass place that will make you feel better," Bibi said. She put her trunk in his mouth to show she was glad he was all right.

Sukari also put her little trunk into Moja's mouth.

"I'll never go there again," Moja whispered.

They arrived at the good grass place at dusk.

A large herd greeted them by touching trunks and rumbling happily.
Sukari ran towards the young elephants, flopping her ears.

Asha, following Bibi's instruction, led Moja to the bitter grass and stood over him while he ate.

Zuri was happy to find acacia leaves. She was nearing twenty-two months—the last month of her pregnancy —and always hungry.

Sukari ate the same flowers, grasses and branches that her mother ate.
Zebras, buffalo and gazelles shared the water hole and the grasses, too.

When the sun got too hot the elephants wallowed in the mud
and showered themselves with water sucked up in their trunks.
Sukari played with her friends while Moja roughhoused
with the young males.

One day Bibi heard the leader of the bull elephants trumpet DANGER. Bibi raised her trunk and sniffed the air. "There is danger," she told her family.

"We must go to Amani, the place of safety."

Amani was a wildlife preserve where men and women who worked there protected wild animals from poachers. But it was several hours away.

On the way they heard the noise of a motor vehicle.
Bibi headed away from the sound toward the bushes.

Just as she spoke, there was a loud bang and then another and another. Bibi fell to her knees.

Men with long guns stood up from the bushes.

Asha raised her trunk and charged trumpeting at the poachers, with her ears folded to attack. The poachers ran back to their jeep.

Then they drove off . Sadly, they would return later for Bibi's ivory tusks.

A ranger from Amani was nearby and heard the shots.

He came to investigate and saw Bibi lying on the ground. He went after the poachers but they got away.

The adult elphants tried to lift
Bibi with their tusks and trunks.
They could not move her.

"Oh Bibi, don't die," Sukari
whispered to herself.

They heard another shot.
Asha rumbled, "Run quickly.
The danger is not over."

"We can't leave Bibi," said Zuri.

"She is gone. Now we must save
our calves," said Asha.

She was the oldest and would
become the new leader.

They moved off. Sukari looked back. Bibi, her grandmother, matriarch of the family, lay still, her ivory tusks gleaming in the evening light.

"Kwaheri, good-bye, kwaheri Grandmother," Sukari said as she followed her mother.

The ranger circled back and from a distance escorted the herd to the safe place.

Now it was up to Asha, Moja's mother, to lead the herd toward the sunset.

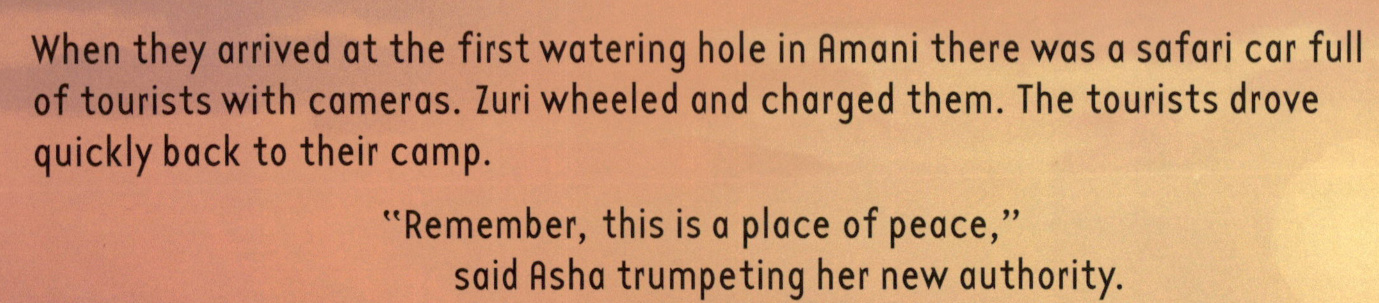

When they arrived at the first watering hole in Amani there was a safari car full of tourists with cameras. Zuri wheeled and charged them. The tourists drove quickly back to their camp.

"Remember, this is a place of peace,"
said Asha trumpeting her new authority.

Sukari was still upset. She and Moja talked for
a long while until at last they both fell asleep.

The next day a new herd arrived at the watering hole.

"We saw the body of your matriarch," one elephant said.
"Her beautiful ivory tusks are gone."

"Then it is safe to go honor her," said Asha.
 She learned from sad experience that poachers
 lost interest in their kill after they took the ivory tusks.

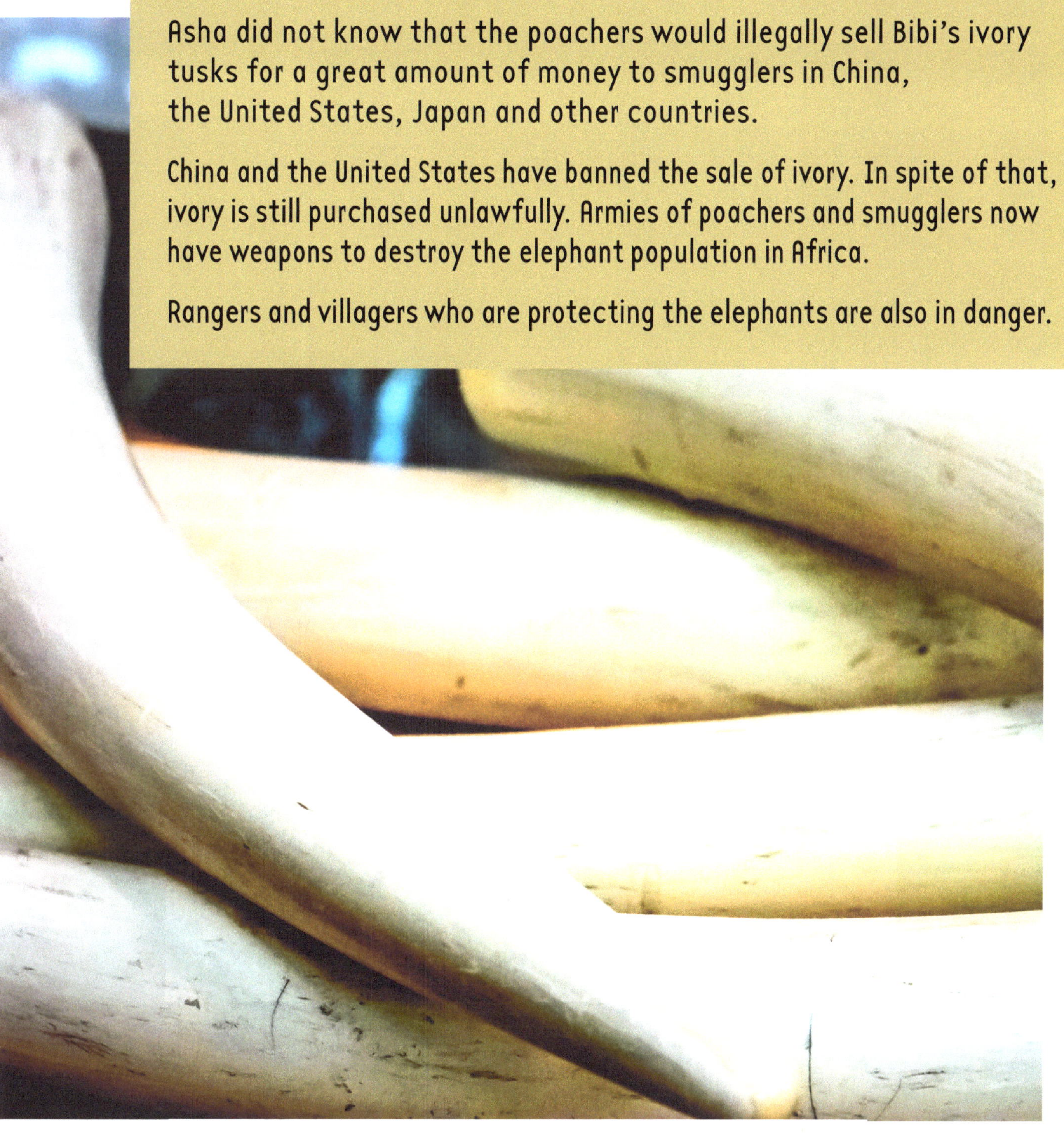

Asha did not know that the poachers would illegally sell Bibi's ivory tusks for a great amount of money to smugglers in China, the United States, Japan and other countries.

China and the United States have banned the sale of ivory. In spite of that, ivory is still purchased unlawfully. Armies of poachers and smugglers now have weapons to destroy the elephant population in Africa.

Rangers and villagers who are protecting the elephants are also in danger.

Zuri led the herd back to where Bibi lay. A circle of vultures and hyenas moved away as they approached.

Zuri raised her trunk and trumpeted sadly as the older
elephants circled Bibi's body and kicked dust on it.

"Kwaheri Bibi, good-bye," Sukari said softly,
then turned to follow the herd back to Amani.

For the next month, Asha moved them from watering hole to open plain and back to watering hole again. The rains made delicious new food grow everywhere. Moja was stuffing almost everything into his mouth.

"He's going to get a stomachache again," Sukari thought.

One day, Sukari noticed a growing bulge
in her mother's belly.

It was a rainy day. Zuri usually loved the feeling of rain as it cooled and cleansed her. But now she went out of the rain into a clump of bushes.

Sukari followed her mother. Zuri stood in the thicket and swung her trunk back and forth.

Later, Asha went into the
bushes where Zuri was.
What could be going on?

Sukari returned just in time
to see a baby elephant
standing under Zuri!

Sukari touched her new baby brother all over with her trunk. He was beautiful.
She ran from the bushes to tell everyone the good news. There was loud and joyful trumpeting from the rest of the family. They named him Wambua, which means "of the rains."

Over the following months,
Sukari helped to teach her
little brother about the
other animals who came
to the watering holes.

She told him about Twiga, the long necked giraffe, who could reach his head even higher in the trees than elephants.

About Swara, the antelope, who runs very fast.

About Tumbill the monkey and his large family.

About Simba, the lion. "Stay away from him. He's dangerous to baby elephants."

Moja's life was changing, too.
He was already spending his nights with the young bulls.

Sukari knew she would stay with her mother and the herd, learn how to take care of the calves, how to find the good grasses and watering holes, and where to go in the dry season. She would trust the rangers who would help protect them from poachers.

Sukari would become a wise elephant and in twenty-five years she would be the mother of a calf or two.

Some day she might even be the new matriarch.

***

ORGANIZATIONS AND ARTICLES THAT HELP SAVE ELEPHANTS IN AFRICA

The David Sheldrick Wildlife Trust
www.sheldrickwildlifetrust.org

The African Wildlife Foundation
www.awf.org

World Wildlife Fund
www.worldwildlife.org

Save the Elephants
info@savetheelephants.org

Thula Thula Game Preserve, Zulu Land, South Africa
www.thulathula.com

The Elephant Sanctuary in Tennessee
www.elephants.com

National Geographic, August 12, 2015
"Tracking the Illegal Tusk Trade"

LAST DAYS a video by Kathryn Bigelow

The New York Times, Tuesday, May 15, 2018
"Research Suggests That the Elephant Walk May Also
Be A Kind of Talk"

Elephant Whisperer
By Lawrence Anthony